ALL ADDICTION 12-STEP PROGRAM WORKBOOK AND JOURNAL FOR MAKING AMENDS

THE HOW AND WHY OF STEPS 8 & 9
FOR
ALCOHOLICS, DRUG ADDICTS, CODEPENDENTS, OVEREATERS, WHATEVER

B&P BOOKWORKS LLC
Publisher of
Butterflies and Paratroopers
Are Not Born With Wings

First Edition Published in the United States

To contact the author: milo@bpbooks.org

ALL ADDICTION 12-STEP PROGRAM
WORKBOOK AND JOURNAL
FOR MAKING AMENDS

Steps Eight and Nine

Step Eight gets only one paragraph in the book from which the fellowship gets its name. The ninth step is nine pages. Yet, one does not outweigh the other.

In Step Eight it says we have a list. We made it when we took inventory. So, does that mean we owe everyone in our inventory an amends? Yes, we do. But not all of them will receive direct amends. That's neither possible nor practical. Thus, we will make most of our amends by changing those behaviors that caused us to say, "I'm sorry" in the first place.

Continuing with eight we get some clear-cut simple directions. (1) We become willing to do what needs to be done to repair the damage caused by living a life on self-will run riot. (2) In reviewing who gets a direct amends we make a drastic self-appraisal. Here we are reminded to make amends for what we did, not what we thought. Approaching someone you knew in fourth grade to remind them that they were fat, stupid, and ugly will do more harm than good. That is if they even remember you. (3) We repair the damage. If we owe money, we pay it back. Also, we inquire if there is something else. (4) When finished we sweep off our side of the street. What does this mean? It means we forgive them for any wrong they may have done. For it is from learning how to forgive others that we learn how to forgive ourselves. And that is what this is all about. (5) If we haven't the will to do this, we ask (pray) until we do. It's from following these directions that we achieve victory over our bondage of self.

Sometimes we hear, all we must do is stop what we are doing. We know that's not true. For now we need more action, because faith without work is death. Not a physical death, but a spiritual one. For only when the spiritual malady is overcome do we straighten out mentally and physically. Make no mistake about it. Each amends made is its own spiritual experience.

Step Nine is not something we just "get around to". If we don't want to make matters worse, then careful contemplation and preparation is necessary. Here, we transform our fourth step inventory into our ninth step reference book.

The causes and conditions for the amends need to be "on point". There is little need to regurgitate the details of your being selfish, dishonest, self-seeking, and afraid. The recipient knows all about what you did or didn't do. Their time is a valuable commodity. Don't waste it.

And what is an amends? Well, it's not only an apology. We're told, a remorseful mumbling that we are sorry doesn't fit the bill at all. Amends require repairing the damage. And this means consequences. And the reason there are consequences is because if you give something away, and it cost you nothing, then what is it worth. Remember, the recipient will be more interested in a demonstration of our goodwill than our talk. What we do speaks louder than anything we say.

Why We Make Amends
Congratulations! You've made a fearless and thorough moral inventory, admitted your defects, and are now ready to go out and clean off your side of the street. This begins the process of recovery where, "we used to think one way, and now we think another," gets turned into action. Thus, to get out of these steps what's intended, you better know what you're doing. For the last thing you want when making an amends is to make matters worse. This workbook helps you turn that fourth step inventory into your ninth step reference book.

So why make amends? Isn't tracking down a bunch of people who don't want to see us just looking for trouble? Why can't we just move on and let bygones be bygones? To answer, let's look at what we get out of it.
- We agreed in the beginning we would go to any length for victory over alcohol.
- If our manner is calm. frank, and open, we will be gratified with the results.
- We find the experience beneficial to us.
- We are trying to put our lives in order.
- We will be able to stand on our feet and look the world in the eye without fear of other people's opinion, or of being found out.

Amend Categories

The directions for the ninth step are specific, not mandatory. We believe that you can't do recovery wrong – only quit. And where do most people give up on themselves? It's balking with completing the ninth. They continue to hold on to those worse items in stock and in time suffer from a lack of spiritual growth. In the Big Book step nine suggests five general categories for making direct amends. These are (Big Book 4th Edition):

1. Business acquaintances and friends (page 76).
2. Financial amends (page 78).
3. Legal (page 78).
4. Domestic troubles (page 80).
5. Family amends (page 82)

How to Use This Workbook

Pull out your fourth step. Flip through it and jot down those people and institutions you owe a direct amends in the pages provided for this. This list is fluid. You can add to, or subtract from, as you pray and meditate about making amends. We suggest you highlight or star those that are the most difficult. These will require consultation and preparation. Remember, the requirement is to make direct amends except when to do so, would injure others.

Read through the amend category checklists. Here you'll find a synopsis of what's suggested in the Big Book. Then, look at that fourth step again and pick out those things that may be applicable to the situation. Feel free to check off and make notes. Look for patterns and develop a specific course of action for each amend. While your behavior may be similar, no two recipients are identical. Your sincerity regarding regret and setting things right is what will matter most to them.

Now that you know the category and have developed a plan let's look at the cause and effects. Here, we are trying to identify and be free of those things that are holding us back. Yes, it is probably true the other party has some responsibility too. We may not be too keen about admitting our faults to them. But we must if we are to achieve sobriety which is clarity of thought. The reason these people are on your list is because you've been carrying them around. If you want to get them off your back, then do something about it. However, a word of caution here. It is essential to leave one word out of every amend you make. And that word is you. As in you did, or if you didn't do.

Now prioritize and time the amend. If a parent is on their deathbed, waste no time. If you need experience, do the easy ones first. However, most amends can be scheduled so you'll have some time to think about the difficulties and complications that may arise. You want to do this right. When you are ready the time will be right. So, relax, take it easy, and don't struggle.

Remember, there may be cases where the other party has no interest in seeing you. Respect that. There is no absolute requirement for a face-to-face conversation if some other communication will do. What you don't want to do, is "amend by ambush". This is where you see someone in the Walmart checkout line, and you jump right into how you were an unfaithful partner. Remember an amend can be more difficult for the receiver than the transmitter. If the time is right, you'll have God by your side, but they may not.

If you need more checklists than provided, feel free to duplicate some. Also, you may want to tear the checklist out and take it along with you as a primer. And if you're interesting in learning more about living life of life's terms, one day at a time, and being happy, joyous, and free then we suggest you take a peek at the author's primary book – Butterflies and Paratroopers Are Not Born With Wings. It is funny, one-of-a-kind, and presents the recovery process in brief, clear, and simple language. Enjoy!

EIGHTH STEP DIRECT AMENDS LIST

NAME OR INSTITUTION	DIFFICULTY LEVEL			TIMING PRIORITY	
	SERIOUS	HARD	EASY	ASAP	IN TIME

EIGHTH STEP DIRECT AMENDS LIST					
	DIFFICULTY LEVEL			TIMING PRIORITY	
NAME OR INSTITUTION	SERIOUS	HARD	EASY	ASAP	IN TIME

Business Acquaintances and Friends

f you're anything like the rest of us, in this category most of your imends reside. This means the cast of characters, and the multitude of trespasses, will each have its own script. Therefore, unlike with some other categories there aren't definitive means or methods on how you clean up your side of the street. Thus, you'll never know what you'll find out about yourself until you begin trudging this road to happy destiny.

n making amends there are misgivings. After all, there are two sides to every story. And yes, they have harmed you as well. So, it's only natural to feel diffident about going to someone to admit the harm you've done to them. That means it's okay to be hesitant about correcting the wrong. But you still have to do it.

We know how to say "sorry". It's that making "things right" we don't have experience with. Thus, it's vital that we understand not only what we are making amends for, but why we are making them. This makes that fourth step inventory our ninth step reference book.

There's no reason to fear making amends. The truth is, we are rarely thrown out of someone's office. However, we do need to take some precautions. First, we don't announce we've got religion. Two, we don't crawl before anyone. Three, we do not criticize or argue. Four, their faults are not discussed. And finally, having made the demonstration we don't look back. It is what it is, and that's that.

Many believe we do this work for the benefit of others. News Flash: most of those in this category could care less if you make amends or not. They have moved on with their lives. So, why then do we make amends? Because we are trying to put our lives in order so we can recover from a seemingly hopeless condition of mind and body. You see, if we are not free of our past, we remain in the bondage of self. Thus, the amends process is the touchstone of, we used to think one way, and now we think another. And once established on such a footing, all sorts of remarkable things begin to happen. We feel new power flow in. We enjoy peace of mind. We discover we can face life successfully. We feel a nearness to our Creator. And we begin to lose our fear of yesterday, today, and tomorrow. And that is why we make amends.

NAME	BUSINESS ACQUAINTANCES AND FRIENDS			
	Where was I			
Nature Of The Wrong	Selfish	Dishonest	Self-seeking	Frightened

Course of action to correct the wrong:

The Nature of the Wrong is	Serious	Difficult	Moderate	Mild
Timeline to Correct the Wrong	Schedule ASAP		As Time Permits	

ADDITIONAL THOUGHTS ON THIS AMENDS:

NAME	BUSINESS ACQUAINTANCES AND FRIENDS			
	Where was I			
Nature Of The Wrong	Selfish	Dishonest	Self-seeking	Frightened

Course of action to correct the wrong:

The Nature of the Wrong is	Serious	Difficult	Moderate	Mild
Timeline to Correct the Wrong	Schedule ASAP		As Time Permits	

ADDITIONAL THOUGHTS ON THIS AMENDS:

NAME	BUSINESS ACQUAINTANCES AND FRIENDS			
	Where was I			
Nature Of The Wrong	Selfish	Dishonest	Self-seeking	Frightened

Course of action to correct the wrong:

The Nature of the Wrong is	Serious	Difficult	Moderate	Mild
Timeline to Correct the Wrong	Schedule ASAP		As Time Permits	

ADDITIONAL THOUGHTS ON THIS AMENDS:

NAME	BUSINESS ACQUAINTANCES AND FRIENDS			
	Where was I			
Nature Of The Wrong	Selfish	Dishonest	Self-seeking	Frightened

Course of action to correct the wrong:

The Nature of the Wrong is	Serious	Difficult	Moderate	Mild
Timeline to Correct the Wrong	Schedule ASAP		As Time Permits	

ADDITIONAL THOUGHTS ON THIS AMENDS:

NAME	BUSINESS ACQUAINTANCES AND FRIENDS			
	Where was I			
Nature Of The Wrong	**Selfish**	**Dishonest**	**Self-seeking**	**Frightened**

Course of action to correct the wrong:

The Nature of the Wrong is	Serious	Difficult	Moderate	Mild
Timeline to Correct the Wrong	Schedule ASAP		As Time Permits	

ADDITIONAL THOUGHTS ON THIS AMENDS:

NAME	BUSINESS ACQUAINTANCES AND FRIENDS			
	Where was I			
Nature Of The Wrong	Selfish	Dishonest	Self-seeking	Frightened

Course of action to correct the wrong:

The Nature of the Wrong is	Serious	Difficult	Moderate	Mild
Timeline to Correct the Wrong	Schedule ASAP		As Time Permits	

ADDITIONAL THOUGHTS ON THIS AMENDS:

NAME	BUSINESS ACQUAINTANCES AND FRIENDS			
	Where was I			
Nature Of The Wrong	Selfish	Dishonest	Self-seeking	Frightened

Course of action to correct the wrong:

The Nature of the Wrong is	Serious	Difficult	Moderate	Mild

Timeline to Correct the Wrong	Schedule ASAP		As Time Permits	

ADDITIONAL THOUGHTS ON THIS AMENDS:

NAME	BUSINESS ACQUAINTANCES AND FRIENDS			
	Where was I			
Nature Of The Wrong	Selfish	Dishonest	Self-seeking	Frightened

Course of action to correct the wrong:

The Nature of the Wrong is	Serious	Difficult	Moderate	Mild
Timeline to Correct the Wrong	Schedule ASAP		As Time Permits	

ADDITIONAL THOUGHTS ON THIS AMENDS:

NAME	BUSINESS ACQUAINTANCES AND FRIENDS			
	Where was I			
Nature Of The Wrong	Selfish	Dishonest	Self-seeking	Frightened

Course of action to correct the wrong:

The Nature of the Wrong is	Serious	Difficult	Moderate	Mild
Timeline to Correct the Wrong	Schedule ASAP		As Time Permits	

ADDITIONAL THOUGHTS ON THIS AMENDS:

NAME	BUSINESS ACQUAINTANCES AND FRIENDS			
	Where was I			
Nature Of The Wrong	**Selfish**	**Dishonest**	**Self-seeking**	**Frightened**

Course of action to correct the wrong:

The Nature of the Wrong is	Serious	Difficult	Moderate	Mild

Timeline to Correct the Wrong	Schedule ASAP		As Time Permits	

ADDITIONAL THOUGHTS ON THIS AMENDS:

NAME	BUSINESS ACQUAINTANCES AND FRIENDS			
	Where was I			
Nature Of The Wrong	Selfish	Dishonest	Self-seeking	Frightened

Course of action to correct the wrong:

The Nature of the Wrong is	Serious	Difficult	Moderate	Mild
Timeline to Correct the Wrong	Schedule ASAP		As Time Permits	

ADDITIONAL THOUGHTS ON THIS AMENDS:

Financial

Contrary to popular belief, financial amends are the easiest to make. You just pay back what you owe. But how do you pay back a thousand dollars? Well, how about twenty dollars a week for a year. And if you can't do that? Then make it ten or even five. The point being, that you begin. For with this amend, postponement is the wrong.

What makes this amend so easy, is we are no longer spending all our money on alcohol, drugs, people, food, or whatever. We get it. But in the past, you found the funds you needed to get what you wanted it so there is no excuse for delay.

Why is it so important to start this amends? Because when we are in debt, we are afraid. We are afraid to answer the phone, open the mail, or even take out the trash. And what are we told? We're told must lose our fear of facing our creditors for we're liable to relapse if we don't. Note that the key word in that phase is "facing". This means it's okay to make the best deal we can. Your creditors don't want to hear any, "but I'm sober now song-and-dance". Our creditors don't what our money. They want their money back.

In in paying them off you'll feel delighted. For nothing earns you self-esteem more than knowing you are being responsible and accountable. They say money can't buy happiness, but paying off a debt will provide you with some much-needed relief from bondage of self.

The hardest hurdles to overcome in recovery is disbelieving the lies you tell yourself. When it comes to financial amends do not make any promises you can't keep. For if you renege on the deal made, you'll not only compound your own shame, guilt, and remorse, but you'll make all of us look bad. Ouch! That's supposed to hurt.

So, what is the financial amend? We pay our bills in full and on time. It doesn't get any simpler than that. Now does it?

	FINANCIAL			
CREDITOR NAME				
What is the dollar amount of the debt?	Credit Card	Utility	Personal	Other

Is this an actual or estimated amount?

Will you pay off this debt lump sum or in payments?

Are you in contact with the creditor?

If so, how much **can you** pay them?

If not in contact with the creditor how will you pay off the debt?

How will you avoid being delinquent on this type of debt in the future?

Having arranged the best deal you can, have you now lost your fear of this creditor?

What have you learned from this experience?

	FINANCIAL			
CREDITOR NAME				
What is the dollar amount of the debt?	Credit Card	Utility	Personal	Other

Is this an actual or estimated amount?

Will you pay off this debt lump sum or in payments?

Are you in contact with the creditor?

If so, how much **can you** pay them?

If not in contact with the creditor how will you pay off the debt?

How will you avoid being delinquent on this type of debt in the future?

Having arranged the best deal you can, have you now lost your fear of this creditor?

What have you learned from this experience?

	FINANCIAL			
CREDITOR NAME				
What is the dollar amount of the debt?	Credit Card	Utility	Personal	Other

Is this an actual or estimated amount?

Will you pay off this debt lump sum or in payments?

Are you in contact with the creditor?

If so, how much **can you** pay them?

If not in contact with the creditor how will you pay off the debt?

How will you avoid being delinquent on this type of debt in the future?

Having arranged the best deal you can, have you now lost your fear of this creditor?

What have you learned from this experience?

	FINANCIAL			
CREDITOR NAME				
What is the dollar amount of the debt?	Credit Card	Utility	Personal	Other

Is this an actual or estimated amount?

Will you pay off this debt lump sum or in payments?

Are you in contact with the creditor?

If so, how much **can you** pay them?

If not in contact with the creditor how will you pay off the debt?

How will you avoid being delinquent on this type of debt in the future?

Having arranged the best deal you can, have you now lost your fear of this creditor?

What have you learned from this experience?

	FINANCIAL			
CREDITOR NAME				
What is the dollar amount of the debt?	Credit Card	Utility	Personal	Other

Is this an actual or estimated amount?

Will you pay off this debt lump sum or in payments?

Are you in contact with the creditor?

If so, how much **can you** pay them?

If not in contact with the creditor how will you pay off the debt?

How will you avoid being delinquent on this type of debt in the future?

Having arranged the best deal you can, have you now lost your fear of this creditor?

What have you learned from this experience?

Legal

If there are two things, we all have in common, it's that when caught, we say, "I didn't do it." And when confronted with the indisputable evidence, then, "It's not my fault."

Not every time we used; did we get into trouble. But evidently, whenever we got in trouble, we were using. So, having legal misfortune is not a rarity among us. And, even if these encounters are not of a criminal nature, civil action, as in divorce, is often somewhere in our repertoire.

In making amends that put us into legal jeopardy it must be kept in mind we have already admitted these things. And while our fifth step is not a get out of jail free card, it is a consideration in deciding what to do about things like this. Reparations and restitution can take innumerable forms. Thus, while it is of paramount importance to be willing to go to any lengths for victory over our addiction, this doesn't mean we should not sink the ship to save the man overboard. Never-the-less, we can be rest assured that regardless of our decision, if we have carefully followed the directions, we will be given the strength and the sanity to do the right thing.

And while on one hand we must not shrink from accountability, on the other we are not to be the hasty and foolish martyr. Especially, if such an action will cause harm to the innocent of those associated with us. And equally important do we not drag, even the guilty, down with us to save our own skin. So, as you can see, this type of amends can be quite complicated. Thus, you best not rush into this matter without the benefit of prayer, meditation, and consultation.

It's also probable that much of this happened long ago. And even though you've turned over a new leaf, no, you didn't get away with it. Instead, you've served your sentence by living with it. There's a reason the legal system has a statute of limitations. Remember, there may be some wrongs we can never fully right. We don't worry about them if we can honestly say to ourselves, we would right them if we could.

TYPE OF TROUBLE	**LEGAL**
	Are you innocent or guilty? Use this space to state your case.

Are you a fugitive or have your head above the water?
Have you fully admitted this in your fifth?
What could the consequences be?
Are you ready and willing to go to any length?
Have you sought guidance using prayer and meditation?
Have you consulted with others who may be involved?
Are you being a hasty and foolish martyr?
How will you make restitution, reparations and reframe from this type of behavior?

TYPE OF TROUBLE	LEGAL
	Are you innocent or guilty? Use this space to state your case.

Are you a fugitive or have your head above the water?

Have you fully admitted this in your fifth?

What could the consequences be?

Are you ready and willing to go to any length?

Have you sought guidance using prayer and meditation?

Have you consulted with others who may be involved?

Are you being a hasty and foolish martyr?

How will you make restitution, reparations and reframe from this type of behavior?

	LEGAL
TYPE OF TROUBLE	Are you innocent or guilty? Use this space to state your case.

Are you a fugitive or have your head above the water?
Have you fully admitted this in your fifth?
What could the consequences be?
Are you ready and willing to go to any length?
Have you sought guidance using prayer and meditation?
Have you consulted with others who may be involved?
Are you being a hasty and foolish martyr?
How will you make restitution, reparations and reframe from this type of behavior?

TYPE OF TROUBLE	LEGAL
	Are you innocent or guilty? Use this space to state your case.

Are you a fugitive or have your head above the water?

Have you fully admitted this in your fifth?

What could the consequences be?

Are you ready and willing to go to any length?

Have you sought guidance using prayer and meditation?

Have you consulted with others who may be involved?

Are you being a hasty and foolish martyr?

How will you make restitution, reparations and reframe from this type of behavior?

	LEGAL
TYPE OF TROUBLE	Are you innocent or guilty? Use this space to state your case.

Are you a fugitive or have your head above the water?

Have you fully admitted this in your fifth?

What could the consequences be?

Are you ready and willing to go to any length?

Have you sought guidance using prayer and meditation?

Have you consulted with others who may be involved?

Are you being a hasty and foolish martyr?

How will you make restitution, reparations and reframe from this type of behavior?

---×---

Domestic Troubles

"We all have sex problems. We'd hardly be human if we didn't." Yet, drinking does complicate sex relations.

Oh boy! Here we go. If we want to talk about self-will run riot, then this is the category for that. However, we can take solace in the realization that no one among us, regardless of addiction, hasn't been mixed up in a fashion we would want advertised. So, rest easy. You're not the first, nor will you be the last, making amends of this sort. Whatever the situation we must do something about it.

Often, just the thought of approaching someone in this category is cause for balking. We know most breakups aren't pretty. In fact, people can be rather fanatical and hysterical when it comes to past sexual relations. And for that reason, we strictly only focus on our own failings.

Also, before proceeding it's imperative that we get down to the causes and conditions for having to make amends of this sort. Thus, we must carefully review what is written in our fourth step inventory/ninth step reference book. And after thoughtful contemplation determine if the exact nature of this wrong meets the "except" clause of the ninth step. And if it does, then the best amends you can make here, is to just leave that someone alone. More than that we cannot do.

And if it is decided to proceed, then next ask yourself, is this the kind of stuff you would want to be reminded of? We have no right to revive nightmares of days-gone-by at the expense of the other party. Amends are not for regurgitating past misdeeds. Instead, we subject each interaction to the test – was it selfish or not.

When making this type of amends it may be best to leave out all the details. And should they bring up the details? Then we suggest you just listen no matter how hard it hurts, or even if it's not true. For it is from these experiences that we will come to understand the absolute necessity to abide by, and grow toward, our newly defined sexual ideal. In other words, we make amends here as we would in any other category. We invite God in and ask Him to direct our attention to what He would have us be. Do this, and the right answer will come.

---×---

	DOMESTIC TROUBLES
Name	What are we going to do about this?

Have you reviewed your 4th step?

Are you in regular and cordial contact with this person?

Does this person hold animosity towards you?

Does this person want to talk to you?

Has this person "moved on" with their life?

Are you ready and willing to go to any length?

What is the motivation for this amends?

What are your expectations?

Have you sought guidance with prayer and meditation?

What items are best left unsaid in this matter?

Are you sorry for what you've done?

What are you willing to give up to make up for and refrain from this type of trouble again?

	DOMESTIC TROUBLES
Name	What are we going to do about this?

Have you reviewed your 4th step?

Are you in regular and cordial contact with this person?

Does this person hold animosity towards you?

Does this person want to talk to you?

Has this person "moved on" with their life?

Are you ready and willing to go to any length?

What is the motivation for this amends?

What are your expectations?

Have you sought guidance with prayer and meditation?

What items are best left unsaid in this matter?

Are you sorry for what you've done?

What are you willing to give up to make up for and refrain from this type of trouble again?

	DOMESTIC TROUBLES
Name	What are we going to do about this?

Have you reviewed your 4th step?

Are you in regular and cordial contact with this person?

Does this person hold animosity towards you?

Does this person want to talk to you?

Has this person "moved on" with their life?

Are you ready and willing to go to any length?

What is the motivation for this amends?

What are your expectations?

Have you sought guidance with prayer and meditation?

What items are best left unsaid in this matter?

Are you sorry for what you've done?

What are you willing to give up to make up for and refrain from this type of trouble again?

	DOMESTIC TROUBLES
Name	What are we going to do about this?

Have you reviewed your 4th step?

Are you in regular and cordial contact with this person?

Does this person hold animosity towards you?

Does this person want to talk to you?

Has this person "moved on" with their life?

Are you ready and willing to go to any length?

What is the motivation for this amends?

What are your expectations?

Have you sought guidance with prayer and meditation?

What items are best left unsaid in this matter?

Are you sorry for what you've done?

What are you willing to give up to make up for and refrain from this type of trouble again?

Name	DOMESTIC TROUBLES
	What are we going to do about this?

Have you reviewed your 4th step?

Are you in regular and cordial contact with this person?

Does this person hold animosity towards you?

Does this person want to talk to you?

Has this person "moved on" with their life?

Are you ready and willing to go to any length?

What is the motivation for this amends?

What are your expectations?

Have you sought guidance with prayer and meditation?

What items are best left unsaid in this matter?

Are you sorry for what you've done?

What are you willing to give up to make up for and refrain from this type of trouble again?

Plenty To Do At Home – Family Amends

Have you ever heard the term "dry drunk"? That's the person who has taken the bit in their teeth and called it quits. Yet, they are a long way from making good. For you can put down the booze, food, drugs, or whatever, and still act like a tornado. So, if your life continues to sow and reap broken hearts, dead relationships, and uprooted affections then there may be something wrong with your spiritual condition.

Recovery is not automatic. We must live life on life's terms one day at a time. This means there is a long period of reconstruction ahead. And nowhere will this be more difficult than on the home front. For it is not only necessary to atone for your sins of commission; the things you did, but for those sins of omission. These are those things you were supposed to do but didn't. These are the hardest to repair. You can't go to your child's play if they now have kids of their own.

And while a remorseful mumbling that we are sorry will not fit the bill, we can take heart in the fact that there may be some wrongs we can never fully right. Thus, instead of wallowing in shame, guilt, and remorse we clean up our side of the street. And in so doing, our disposition toward others will become sensible, tactful, considerate, and humble. It's our behaviors that will convince them we have changed more than our words.

In making this type of amends you'll be vulnerable to the character defects of those closest to you. Yes, on hearing your amends they may say, "forget it". Don't believe them. The wounds run deep, and some are scarred for life. Beware to keep your expectations in check. Trying to force the issue is to wrest, or take by force, the happiness that is not given. Yet, there is some truth in the adage that time heals old wounds. Never forget the amends is about you. In making amends, you get better. And in getting better you'll soon be amazed that you are happy, joyous, and free.

With each amend made, you'll feel new power flow in. You'll enjoy peace of mind, discover you can face life successfully, and lose your fear of yesterday, today, and tomorrow.

FAMILY

Who this amends for, and what damage is to be repaired?

What is your sobriety/clean/abstinence date?

How difficult will it be to make this amends?

Do you think you are ready to make this amends?

Is the recipient ready to hear your amends?

How did you determine you and they are ready?

What is your timing and expectations for this amends?

What will the consequences be?

A review of your Fourth Step regarding the recipient revealed what about them, and their relationship with you? Are there any issues that are best left unsaid?

FAMILY

Who this amends for, and what damage is to be repaired?

What is your sobriety/clean/abstinence date?

How difficult will it be to make this amends?

Do you think you are ready to make this amends?

Is the recipient ready to hear your amends?

How did you determine you and they are ready?

What is your timing and expectations for this amends?

What will the consequences be?

A review of your Fourth Step regarding the recipient revealed what about them, and their relationship with you? Are there any issues that are best left unsaid?

FAMILY

Who this amends for, and what damage is to be repaired?

What is your sobriety/clean/abstinence date?

How difficult will it be to make this amends?

Do you think you are ready to make this amends?

Is the recipient ready to hear your amends?

How did you determine you and they are ready?

What is your timing and expectations for this amends?

What will the consequences be?

A review of your Fourth Step regarding the recipient revealed what about them, and their relationship with you? Are there any issues that are best left unsaid?

FAMILY

Who this amends for, and what damage is to be repaired?

What is your sobriety/clean/abstinence date?

How difficult will it be to make this amends?

Do you think you are ready to make this amends?

Is the recipient ready to hear your amends?

How did you determine you and they are ready?

What is your timing and expectations for this amends?

What will the consequences be?

A review of your Fourth Step regarding the recipient revealed what about them, and their relationship with you? Are there any issues that are best left unsaid?

FAMILY

Who this amends for, and what damage is to be repaired?

What is your sobriety/clean/abstinence date?

How difficult will it be to make this amends?

Do you think you are ready to make this amends?

Is the recipient ready to hear your amends?

How did you determine you and they are ready?

What is your timing and expectations for this amends?

What will the consequences be?

A review of your Fourth Step regarding the recipient revealed what about them, and their relationship with you? Are there any issues that are best left unsaid?

FAMILY

Who this amends for, and what damage is to be repaired?

What is your sobriety/clean/abstinence date?

How difficult will it be to make this amends?

Do you think you are ready to make this amends?

Is the recipient ready to hear your amends?

How did you determine you and they are ready?

What is your timing and expectations for this amends?

What will the consequences be?

A review of your Fourth Step regarding the recipient revealed what about them, and their relationship with you? Are there any issues that are best left unsaid?

FOURTH STEP INVENTORY NOTEBOOK SERIES $5.99 each

Each fifty-page notebook provides the "mechanics" for doing the Fourth Step. These 8x11 "fill-in-the-blank" notebooks relieve the writer of having to rewrite the questions for each interrogatory. This allows you to get down to causes and conditions without breaking concentration. These notebooks save time and makes reading the fifth step easy.

·Fourth Step Inventory Resentments
·Fourth Step Inventory Fear
·Fourth Step Inventory Sex

TWELVE STEP WORKBOOK SERIES $6.99 each

The Twelve Steps is a program of action, design for living, and process of recovery. There is a means and method to staying sober, and that's what this series is about. In these workbooks the Big Book is broken down into clear-cut simple directions. Included with the text there are "check on learning" quizzes which makes comprehension and retention easy. Everything you need to know about the Big Book is here.

·Step Zero -The Forwards. Appendices, Bill and Bob
·Step One – The Doctor's Opinion & More About Alcoholism
·Step Two – We Agnostics & There Is A Solution
·Steps Three and Four – How It Works
·Steps Five, Six, and Seven – Into Action (Part 1)
·Steps Eight, Nine, Ten and Eleven – Into Action (Part 2)
·Steep Twelve – Working With Others
·The 13th Step
·Collateral Damage – To Wives, The Family Afterwards, and To Employers
·But For The Grace of God – Vision for You

THE 4TH STEP HOW AND WHY SERIES $6.99 each

The Fourth Step Inventory is a three-part process: Resentment, Fear, and Sex. Each has its own set of questions. These workbooks provide the reader with how and why we do the 4th Step.

·Resentments – What We Like
·Fear – Why We Are Like That
·Sex – Why It's Important to Change